POEMS
For All Occasions

POEMS
For All Occasions

Written By:
TRINA TRICHE

XULON PRESS

Xulon Press
2301 Lucien Way #415
Maitland, FL 32751
407.339.4217
www.xulonpress.com

© 2017 by Trina Triche

All rights reserved solely by the author. The author guarantees all contents are original and do not infringe upon the legal rights of any other person or work. No part of this book may be reproduced in any form without the permission of the author. The views expressed in this book are not necessarily those of the publisher.

Printed in the United States of America.

Trina Triche
P. O. Box 504
Ama, LA 70031

Email: trinattriche@yahoo.com

ISBN-13: 9781545617649

DEDICATION

Thanks be to God for the gift to write and express myself in a manner pleasing to Him. This book of poetry is a collection of thoughts, and the result of prayer. I dedicate this book to all those who prayed for me. When the doctors thought it was over, God said, "Not so." And now, because of the effective prayers of the righteous, I am still here and able to publish my work.

Thank you Irving Pierre Sr., my grandfather, Mr. and Mrs Eldridge and Sherron Triche, my parents, and Terrell (Millicent), Tracy, Tyrus (Dana), Troy, and Trent (Christy), my siblings and their wives, for your special acts of love and service. Thank you aunts, nieces, nephews and cousins. This book is published because of all of you.

Finally, I dedicate this book to all the people who think they can't. With God, you can. Nothing is impossible with Him.

TABLE OF CONTENTS

Witness	1
Happy New Year Rhyme	2
African American	3
Black History	4
Where Ya At Dare Black Moses?	5
Friendship Poem	7
Happy Valentine Day	8
For Your Eyes Only	9
Especially For You	10
The Resurrection	11
Happy Easter	12
Happy Mothers Day	13
I Am Women	14
For Ladies Only	15
Hero	16
Especially For You Dad	17
Dad You Are Unique	18
Happy Father's Day Greetings	19
The King	20
Overcomer	21
Happy Fourth of July	22
Just When You Need Him the Most	23
Trick or Treat	24
Make A Healthy Choice Today	25
Happy Thanksgiving	26
Thank You	27
Season's Greeting	28
Merry Christmas	29
Salvation Prayer	30

Witness

You don't know my
name.
My face you can't see,
but there is something inside compelling me
to be a person of
integrity,
full of compassion and
love—
to shine as a light,
and glorify God
up-above;
to be a witness in the
earth
so that others will see,
that there is a creative
force,
and He is guiding me;
to do good and live
right—
to save the lost
to the blind give sight;
to clothe the naked
and help the poor,
to pray for the sick
and so much more…
My name you don't
know;
my face you can't see,
but my God is in control,
and He is watching over
me.

John 3:16

Happy New Year Rhyme

God has been good.
Oh, yes He has,
and this New Year
will be as good as the past.
I started the year off right
with one quick rhyme.
I have things to do;
I won't waste my time;
I am on the run.
I am no joke.
I can't stand around
just playing with folks.
Things are moving fast;
and people are driving slow.
Please get out of my way;
I have places to go.
You can play games,
if that's what you do.
It's your world;
live your life for you.
As for me and my house,
we're going to walk with God;
we are raising our hands,
and we are singing out loud.
I am hype today,
God is leading the way.
I am stepping high;
I will live and not die.
I am determined to win;
that's all on my mind.
The best is yet to come;
and the crown is mine.

AFRICAN-AMERICAN

African-American is not my name; it is who I am.

African-American is not my continent;
it is my connection to my homeland.

African-American is not my weakness; it is my strength from
which derives my confidence and my convictions.

African-Americans are not powerless; they are powerful, and can
conquer any man-made obstacle that stands in their way.

African-Americans are not underachievers, but rather,
over-comers, who have laughed in the face of adversity and
achieved prominence in a land not their own.

African-Americans are not my enemy; they are my friends.

Black History

You captured us, and took us from our native land.
You brought us here on boats, placing shackles around our hands.
America, the land of the free, is the song you sing,
But for the black man in America, freedom didn't ring.
You sold us like produce, separated us from our families;
You changed our name, our language,
you raped and beat us, on demand.
You used us like a tool, to build America the beautiful,
even though it was not our land, we still made it fruitful.
The horror blacks endured, at the hands of the white man,
will never be justified, redeemed, or morally explained.
Nevertheless, the rules of America, has changed for the black man.
Now my question is, will America allow history, to repeat itself again?
Stand up, speak out, and vote; let your voice be heard.
Insist that black history be taught in schools, to all boys and girls.
Then there will be peace and unity, when we all understand, black history.

Where Ya At Dare Black Moses

Where ya at dare black Moses?
What you doing whit dem slaves?
Who dat waiting in the waters?
Now let them slaves behave.

Massars gonna catch em,
gonna bring dem back,
and whoop dem too.
Better leave dem slaves alone
black Moses,
before Massar whip you.

Where ya at dare black Moses?
Who you got dare singing a song?
Leave dem slaves alone
black Moses.
Let dem stay where dey belong.

Don't cause no trouble;
trouble round here ain't hard to find.
Those slaves gonna pay.
Massar's gonna whip dey behind.
Then what you gonna do
black Moses,
when all is said and done?
You better buy you some tennis shoes.
You better run, run, run.
Dey catch you,
child you gonna burn.

Dey not gonna put you in no grave;
dey gonna put you in an urn.
Yeah, you gonna be a treasure;
you gonna be a treasure from the hunt.
Da one that catch you black Moses,
dey gonna have some fun, fun, fun.

Dey gonna have your name in the paper.
Dey gonna have your picture too.
Dey gonna say God has given them favor,
because He let dem capture you.

Ain't no tellin what the people will do;
what commotion will come, because they caught you.
But somethins gonna happen;
you best believe that;
you da prize capture;
you da big black cat.

Where ya going dare black Moses,
up to heaven's highway?
What do you think St. Peter,
or Jesus gonna say?
Will dey say, "Well done; girl you did good."
Will dey say, "You saved others, just like others should?"
Will dey give you a robe
and a fancy crown?
Where ya going dare black Moses?
Are you heaven bound?

FRIENDSHIP POEM

What's shakin n' bakin?
Is the world still quakin?
Are you movin or losin?
Time that is—

What's healing?
You feeling me?
Where ya going?
Are you soaring?
I am tired of this?

Talkin or walkin?
Which is it?
Do you swim fish?
Make a wish.
That's it!
Give your life to Christ

Romans 10:13

Happy Valentine Day

Love is in the air,
flowers everywhere.
Chocolate is in the store;
it's time to buy more.
Time is winding down;
no time to clown.
Get the gift please,
then get down on your knees.
Ask the question on time,
"Will you be my valentine?"

FOR YOUR EYES ONLY

You are the badest of the bad.
You're the sugar and the spice.
You're the finest leading lady,
and you're three times as nice.
You're the honey for the bee.
You're the sand around the sea.
You're the dove in the sky,
and you are the apple of my eyes.
You're the song in my heart.
You're fine, and you're smart.
You're the peace in my mind,
and you're the best that I could find.
That's why I love you.

ESPECIALLY FOR YOU

Boy, if I believed in luck,
you would be my lucky star.
If I were searching for a king,
I would know that's who you are.
When I needed a friend,
you stepped up to the plate,
and I ate, I ate, I ate....
When things fall apart,
you can touch my heart.
I miss you so much;
you're the dream I can't touch.
I know you are there;
I feel your presence everywhere.
You have the gentleness of a dove;
your works demonstrate your love.
You have courage, and you are brave.
Only you can make me behave.
You have been tried,
and you are true;
that's why I will always love you.

THE RESURRECTION

He hung His head.
My Savior was dead.
With His arms stretched wide,
blood running from His side;
I cried, I cried, I cried.

Then down He came.
He lost His fame.
They laid Him to rest.
He was the best.
When I thought
of how He died,
I cried, I cried, I cried.

The sun was rising,
another day.
The prophet is gone;
the people would say.
No more healings
in the streets;
Just the followers,
and their hurting feet.
When I thought
that He had lied;
I cried, I cried, I cried.

But then a rumbling,
I heard in the ground.
People were running
all around.
Screaming and yelling
He isn't there.
Dancing and singing
like they didn't care.
I started to look up
in the sky.
My Savior's risen
I thought with pride;
then I cried, I cried, I cried.

HAPPY EASTER

Easter Bunny
what's so funny?
You're hopping around
like a circus clown.
Yeah, you have the candy,
and the Easter egg,
but I have Jesus Christ.
who rose from the dead.
Happy Resurrection Celebration

HAPPY MOTHERS DAY

Wishing your special day is great.

Wishing your special day is grand.

Wishing you receive the best gifts of love.

from all your number one fans.

Wishing your day is a happy one.

Wishing you enjoy family and friends.

Wishing you a day of peace and contentment,

now and throughout the year.

I AM WOMAN

I am woman
hear me roar,
and on eagles wings
I will soar—
to heights unknown
and over valleys wide;
I will not fear;
God is on my side.
I am walking tall
with my head
held high.
I'm moving forward,
and I won't be denied.
Fulfilling purpose,
my destiny to achieve;
my trust is in God;
I do believe.
All things are possible;
I will not fail.
My enemies are
defeated.
I Will Prevail!

For Ladies Only

Hey girl,
you're on top of the world.
Stand on your tip toes,
only heaven knows,
how far you can go.
You are the star of the show.
The moon, the sun—
you're the only one,
who can do what you do.
Now walk the walk,
and do you.

Hey girl,
have some fun.
You are glowing my dear.
Don't walk in fear.
You're the cream of the crop,
and you can't be stopped.
You're the diamond in the coal.
Don't cover it up;
demonstrate that you're the gold.

Hey girl.

HERO

The battle has been long,
and the fight I didn't quit.
The struggle has been hard,
but the war I must win.
There are others who are hoping that I stay the course –
so many can rejoice,
in the blessed hope.
That tomorrow is always better,
the future as bright as can be.
They're counting on my perseverance,
so we can have victory.

To God be the Glory!

ESPECIALLY FOR YOU DAD

Thank you dad for staying.
Thank you dad for praying.
Thank you dad for loving.
Thank you dad for covering.
Thank you dad for smiling.
Thank you dad for crying.
Thank you dad for giving.
Thank you dad; you're still living.
Thank you dad for all that you do.
Thank you dad, I'll always love you.
Happy Father's Day

DAD YOU ARE UNIQUE

Fathers are forever.
Fathers are for keep.
Fathers are for telling everyone
how special you are to me.
Happy Father's Day

HAPPY Father's Day Greetings

Wanted

House Dad

Single and Free

Experienced in love and work.

Has no need to be a jerk.

For more information contact me by email:

Happy Father's Day

The King

I am the King of my castle,
and I am the King of the hill.
I don't mean to brag,
but I'm the ultimate thrill.

I have the mind of a leader;
I have a heart of gold.
I am a mover and shaker;
I'm like a rock, and I roll.

The women smile when they see me.
The men don't like what I do.
I tell them I'm filled with God's love,
and I'm not hating on you.

I don't change like a butterfly,
but I'm like honey to a bee.
Yes, I fly like an eagle,
and all eyes are on me.

I like to run real fast,
and I won't covet your place.
So don't get in my way;
I have to finish my race.

I'll wear a robe on my back.
I'll put a crown on my head.
I'll place a ring on my finger,
and no, I won't be dead.

I'm going to walk through the gates;
I'm going to look for the sign.
And when I see I'm in heaven,
I'm going to lose my mind.

The angels will all bow down;
all in heaven will sing,
because I've given up my life on earth,
and now I am living with the KING.

OVERCOMER

It's fireworks;
no peace on earth.
You know what to do,
and God is watching you.
Now don't miss your moment;
it may not come again.
You must make up your mind,
and be released from sin.

Do good to others;
don't hate your brothers.
The world is your playground;
don't mess around.
Continue to seek God's face,
and reject all doubt;
God's amazing grace
will help you out.

Your purpose is waiting;
you cannot fail.
You've been predestined;
you will prevail.
No need to fear;
God is always near.
Accept Jesus Christ,
and you will have a new life.

Happy Fourth of July

Fireworks popping all through the sky;
red, white, and blue are the colors we buy.
Acknowledging our independence in a glorious way;
never forgetting the struggles that led to the day.
It stands for our freedom and justice for all;
it acknowledges the bravery and the American call,
to pursue life and liberty and happiness too;
seeking peace with all men is what we do.
One nation under God is our solemn cry,
as we celebrate our independence on the Fourth of July.

Just When You Need Him the Most

When there is no room in the Inn,
and no travel companion to take you,
or walk with you,
where you need to go,
then look up my friends;
that's just when you need Him the most.

He is always there in the darkest of night.
He shows you He cares,
as He turns your darkness to light.
When all else fails,
and there is nowhere to go,
go down on your knees in prayer,
and lift up your voice.
That's just when you need Him the most.

A word, a song, a verse of Scripture will do,
just know that the Savior loves and cares for you,
and He will carry you through.

Through the storm and through the pain,
the laughter and the shame,
in the good and in the bad,
in the ugly and the sad.
Everybody's looking for a neighbor;
someone they can call friend.
Look up to Jesus,
on Him you can depend.
Just when you need Him the most.....

Trick or Treat

Are you the trick,
because I'm the treat.
I'm the candy
that won't harm your teeth.
I eat the apples
without the stick.
I drink plenty of water,
and I don't get sick.
I play by the rules;
I get good grades in school.
I'm the best of the crop;
I'm the icing on top,
and I like it that way;
that's why I'm here to stay.
Trick or Treat!

Make a Healthy Choice Today

You are who you are,
because of the choices that you make.
So make healthy choices,
and begin the act today.
You smoke?
No joke.
You drink?
Just think,
of what will come your way.
Do you know how important it is,
to exercise every day?
Don't cry, "I'm alive."
No jive. Then why
do you feel bad I say?
Because of the bad choices
that you continuously choose to make.
For heaven's sake,
give me a break,
and do what's right my friend.
That's how you will win,
a healthy life, and live abundantly.
It's never too late.
Jot down this date,
and live a healthy life until the end.

Happy Thanksgiving

Are you in a hurry?
Don't you worry.
Are you feeling ill?
Take a pill.
Are you feeling down?
Don't frown.
Are you all alone?
Use the phone,
and remember this—
God is still on the throne.
Happy Thanksgiving

Thank You

Thank you for caring.
Thank you for sharing.
Any gifts of love,
thank you for bearing,
another man's burden,
and giving him hope,
that tomorrow is
always brighter,
so today he can cope-
with any tribulation,
that may come his way.
God is on the throne, and
He watches us every day.
God Bless You

SEASON'S GREETING

Choirs are singing.
Bells are ringing.
Children are playing.
Christians are praying,
and everybody's saying,
"Wishing you a Merry Christmas
and a Prosperous New Year."

Merry Christmas

Born in a manger was our God,
sent from above.
Dying on a cross
displayed His infinite love.
Tis the season of great joy;
just remember the Christ,
while you play with your toys.
Tis the season of great cheer.
Wishing you love
throughout the New Year.

**Wishing you a very Merry Christmas
and a Happy New Year**

SALVATION PRAYER

Holy, Holy, Holy
Jesus came lowly.
Born in a manager,
and lived among strangers.
Gave up His life;
He was the crucified Christ.
And because I believe the story,
of Jesus who came from glory
I am saved, saved, saved.
Romans 10:9-10

www.ingramcontent.com/pod-product-compliance
Lightning Source LLC
LaVergne TN
LVHW011901060526
838200LV00054B/4457